T0129932

Gumbo

Gumbo

A Recipe for Righteousness

Naisha Cooper

authorHOUSE®

AuthorHouse™
1663 Liberty Drive
Bloomington, IN 47403
www.authorhouse.com
Phone: 1 (800) 839-8640

Gumbo: A Recipe for Righteousness
© 2015 Naisha Cooper. All rights reserved.
Hair/Makeup: Naisha Cooper
Photography: Elle Mouton, [silent.eye] photography
Public Relations: Kashanna Bradford {www.GlamHustlePR.com}
Project Management: Kim Sewell {www.VirtuouslyDone.com}

Published by AuthorHouse   05/20/2015

ISBN: 978-1-5049-1017-0 (sc)
ISBN: 978-1-5049-1016-3 (e)

Library of Congress Control Number: 2015906979

Print information available on the last page.

This book is printed on acid-free paper.

The views expressed in this work are solely those of the author
and do not necessarily reflect the views of the publisher, and the
publisher hereby disclaims any responsibility for them.

Acknowledgements

To God; my parents, Henry and Helen; my children, D'Henrei, Dacien and A'naisha; my sisters, Kshanski and Taryla; my closest confidants, best friends and clients; and those who have caused pain, disappointment and discouragement - through this I've learned perseverance.

To all who believe, trusted and protected my gift and all who read this book, may its contents satisfy your hunger and quench your thirst.

Contents

Introduction

Gumbo is the official cuisine of Louisiana. It is a flavorful stew which features a number of ingredients, such as okra, which hailed from Africa; andouille, which originated in France; seafood from the Gulf of Mexico and creole seasoning from the south. If you "google" gumbo, you will find hundreds of recipes with a variety of ingredients, but it is the roux, seasoning and meat which gives the dish its identity. The roux is created by stirring flour and oil (or butter) over heat. When the roux reaches the desired color and consistency, it is seasoned with chopped bell pepper, onion and celery. Water (or stock) is poured into the roux and after it has simmered a while, the meat is added to the pot to marinate until the gumbo is complete. The end result is a savory dish that is unlike any other.

If you expected a well-written gumbo recipe, with a list of ingredients, pre-prep instructions, cooking temperatures and exact measurements, you are looking in the wrong book. Metaphorically speaking, the gumbo that I refer to represents a unique mixture of circumstances, trials, tribulations and experiences that make you who you are. Like gumbo, you are a culmination of everything that has transpired in your life. The ingredients in your gumbo might be different from your neighbor, because she uses oil and you use butter. You may prefer shrimp and okra in your gumbo, but your friend puts chicken and sausage in hers, simply because that's what she had in her freezer or maybe that's all she can afford.

Just like the ingredients in gumbo will be different from cook to cook, life experiences will vary from woman to woman. I am no different. My unique experiences created a pot of gumbo that tells my story. I was raised in a middle class two-parent home with two sisters. I had a normal and healthy upbringing, but at the age of 16, I was forced into motherhood. I obtained my GED and enrolled in cosmetology school. I got married in my 20's and had two more children - one which has a disability (autism). After enduring mental and physical abuse in my marriage, I decided to get a divorce. Seven years later, I remarried (the same man) in an attempt to be a family again for the children. Ironically, the remarriage proved that we were better off apart, so we divorced again shortly thereafter!

The ingredients in my gumbo may seem to be a plethora of trials and tribulations, but if you stir the pot, you will discover that I accepted Jesus Christ as Lord and Savior at the age of 21, opened my first salon at the age of 22 and became an ordained minister at the age of 34. Even in the midst of divorce, depression and disabilities, God was with me. He supplied my needs and my family is truly blessed! I am not boasting, but I am thankful that God preserved me. I have survived what many have succumbed to. I will never be ashamed of where I've been, because eyes haven't seen where I'm going! I tell my story, because others will see God in it.

This pot of "Gumbo" has been marinating inside me for a long time. I have read my Bible, prayed and written in journals for many years. I wrote most of this book during my quiet time with God, but I also remember writing when my body was in pain and while I was on vacation with my family. Parts of this book were written when my pillow was drenched with tears and even as I waited in a courthouse for a restraining order. When I felt like giving up on everything, I heard God tell me to keep going and He kept sending people to get a portion of the "Gumbo" I had. I didn't write this book because I've reached a place of perfection, but I wrote it to share the recipe that God gave to me.

God wants you to grow closer to Him through daily worship, study and prayer. This book is divided into the 3 core components of gumbo (roux, seasoning and meat) with 7 instructions in each section. If you complete 1 instruction per day, you will have a flavorful pot of "Gumbo" in 21 days. As you read this book, please take every word into consideration. Read the scriptures and write down the things that resonate in your spirit. As you "let it marinate," consider yourself and apply the lesson to your daily life. Don't just say the "prayer," pray the prayer. The prayers of the righteous are powerful and effective (James 5:16).

God wants you to seek His righteousness the way that you desire food when you're hungry and water when you're thirsty. I can't guarantee that you will gain a house, car, husband or a dog after you read this book, but I guarantee if you go to God honestly and fervently concerning your life and obey His instructions, He will add the things you need (Matthew 6:33). This "Gumbo" is ready in season and out of season to fill you up, feed your soul, renew your mind and strengthen your walk with God. Grab a bowl - so that you may taste and see that God is good! Bon Appétit.

Blessed are those who hunger and thirst for righteousness,
for they shall be filled.
Matthew 5:6

Roux

/ roo /

The foundation of a gumbo;
A mixture of flour and oil (or butter)
stirred over heat.

Go to God as Clay

But now, O Lord, You are our Father; we are the clay, and You are our Potter; we are all the work of Your hand. Isaiah 64:8

Have you ever seen a beautiful piece of pottery? You admire its delicate texture, pleasing color and refined sculpture, but before it became a masterpiece, it was a lump of clay. The Potter places the clay on His wheel, opens the center with the pressure of His thumb, smoothes the sides with His hands and shapes the clay into a design. Slowly but surely, the piece is formed and allowed to dry. The excess clay is cut away and the pottery is placed in excruciating heat to harden. The end result is a magnificent work of art.

There are several times in the Bible where the analogy of the Potter and the clay can be found. In Genesis, the Potter spoke the world into existence, molded the Heavens and Earth and formed man from dirt. As the Creator, the Potter has the authority to do whatever He deems necessary to make His creation better. The clay has absolutely nothing to do with the plans of the Potter. It's just clay. He just needs a pliable lump to accomplish His purpose and plan. Think about that - He's the Potter. You're the clay. What has He designed you for? What were you created to do?

The Potter knew what His intentions were before He formed you in your mother's womb. He knows your habits, addictions, rejections and bad decisions. He also knows your potential, resiliency and what you will overcome. He knows the things you don't share with others and the things you've tried to forget. He takes His time and never rushes the process - even though some changes are immediate. Some issues are a struggle that you may continue to go through, but the timing belongs to God. Some things only God can put in you or take away; and just like the Potter uses the water and the wheel, God uses His Word to shape us in righteousness (II Timothy 3:16). The Word reforms, cleanses, purifies and helps us when adversity comes.

When we yield to the Potter for change in our lives, a reshaping takes place. It isn't comfortable, but it's necessary. The Potter knew that the clay had subtle imperfections and impurities, but that didn't prevent Him from molding it. No matter how much dirt and grit is in the clay, He still uses it. No matter what you're going through, what you've been through or what's to come, the Potter has need of you. He can take a broken vessel and make a wonderful work of art.

The Potter holds us in His hands and molds us through different experiences. As we go through this journey of life, He gives us the choice to become clay in His hands. We can go to the Potter with our cracks and brokenness and He will make something beautiful. Even if we've made a mess of things by choices and judgments, the Potter can repair and bring healing so we will display His glory.

Go to God as clay. Allow Him to create a clean heart and right spirit in you. Let Him open up the things that have you closed off and bound. As the shaping process happens, trust that the kinks are being worked out – even if it doesn't feel good. The heat may be turned all the way up in your situation and a few imperfections may still be visible; but when you come out, you will be a masterpiece -because God is the Potter and you are the clay.

Let it Marinate

We have absolutely nothing to do with the plans of the Potter. He does not need our permission to mold and shape us. The Potter will place us in heated situations and we wonder what's the reason or purpose. If you feel like you're in a furnace, it is because God is burning out the impurities and imperfections. Some of us have the audacity to get upset with God when we go through this process, but who are we to quarrel with the one who is the Maker? We are just potsherd - a piece of broken pottery (Isaiah 45:9). It is not easy being molded, but when the clay is placed in the furnace, it is to perfect its shape and soundness. Even if you feel like you've been in the fire too long, know that the Potter never leaves or forsakes His clay. He will complete what He started.

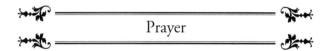

Prayer

Thank You for molding and shaping me into the person You created me to be. Thank You for bringing me out of situations that caused me pain and frustration. Because of Your grace and mercy, I became much stronger in the end. Cleanse my heart of everything that is not of You and use me for Your purpose. In the name of Jesus - I pray. Amen.

As for me, I shall behold Your face in righteousness;
when I awake, I shall be satisfied with Your likeness.
Psalm 17:15

Know Your Father

Father of the fatherless and protector of widows is God in His holy habitation. Psalm 68:5

Growing up, I have the fondest memories of my Dad. He provided, protected and supported whatever my sisters and I did. When I became a teenage mother, my Dad (with no regret) became the father to my son. As a single parent, I learned the balance that a father brings to the equation. Even though my Mom was the main disciplinarian, when she yelled my Dad's name, we knew it was serious. When I became an adult I realized that everyone did not have the type of father we had – a father who put Christmas toys together, gave us piggy back rides, took us on family vacations and loved us unconditionally.

God chose to relate to mankind the language of family. He could have described Himself as a Ruler, Boss or Magistrate, but He chose the word Father – because even if you didn't have a physical father, you have an idea (even if it is vague) of their role in the lives of their children. We all have an innate need to be loved, cherished and valued by an earthly father, but even when they don't, God will. When He created the

Father, He created Him with you in mind- that all your needs and provisions come from Him.

As I think about my experiences with my Dad, I can't help but think about my relationship with my heavenly Father. Just as we have the DNA of our biological father, we have the same DNA as God the Father because He created us in His image. If your mother or father has forsaken you, God will pick you up (Psalm 24:10); but you must have a relationship with Him.

Do you want to have a relationship with God? In order to do so, you must first go through His Son - Jesus. He said, "I am the way and the truth and the life. No one comes to the Father except through Me" (John 14:6). Another person can't stand proxy for your father - no man, habit or addiction. Some will use this as an excuse for certain behaviors, while others use a hard exterior and never acknowledge their absence. Due to God's natural order, that void will eventually be filled – and sometimes we fill it with the wrong person or thing. God the Father wants to fill that void. He wants to be the lover of your soul, your protector and provider. He wants to be the one you rely on for strength - whether you had a physical father or not.

Let it Marinate

How do you view your father? Do your children have a relationship with their father? Has that image shaped your views or ideas about men and if so, how can you change that? The solution is to go to God, seek to know Him and

His plan for your life. There are many dynamics to God, but to be His child you must acknowledge and accept His role as Father.

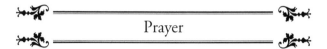

Prayer

Lord, You've been a Father to me when I didn't even understand. Today, I ask that You search my heart and remove everything that is not of You. Remove all the things that I've thought about men - every negative word I've said about my father or my children's father. I want to know You in this manner so that I can be the woman You created me to be. In the name of Jesus, I pray. Amen.

Full of splendor and majesty is His work,
and His righteousness endures forever.
Psalm 111:3

Build Your House

The wisest of women builds her house, but folly with her own hands tears it down. Proverbs 14:1

The most important title you bear before any other is that of a woman. When God created her from Adam's rib, He called her "woman" - not wife, daughter, friend or mother. Before you receive any of those titles, you must know the role of the woman.

A true woman is not to be defined by style, culture, smell or personality. A true woman is one who wakes up every morning faced with a ton of decisions; and despite what the world is telling her, she chooses to make the right choice. She stands by what she believes, realizes what she deserves and doesn't settle for less. She is honest, loyal, 100% faithful and puts up with far more than she should. A true woman gets back up and fights for what she wants time and time again, even though she's tried before and lost. She is understanding and patient, yet abrasive and takes the bull by the horns. She gives respect and expects it in return. You can look in the eyes of a true woman and see confidence and compassion. If she's single, she's still building her life, looking ahead and maintaining her being. If she's married, she brings good to those around her, the children call her blessed and her husband understands that she keeps everything fluid and in order.

Wisdom is a gift from God. It is not developed overnight, but through life's journey. Women should always prioritize according to importance and the home environment should be on the top of the list. When your home life is balanced, it helps you to balance other areas of your life. There is no way you can have chaos at home and it not affect other aspects of your life. Building a house takes planning. You must count up the costs and make sure that you have what it takes on the inside.

Your body is your temple. What goes in it or on it helps others identify you. Your market value is assessed according to you. Proverbs 11:6 says, The righteousness of the upright delivers them, but the treacherous are taken captive by their lust. Can you honestly say that you are building your life, relationships, career, security and your family or have you been acting foolishly by mismanaging your funds, neglecting your responsibilities and sowing into carnal pleasures?

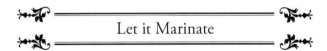
Let it Marinate

Read Proverbs 31 in its entirety. The woman was advising her son (Lemule) on the type of woman that was priceless. Are you a treasure or trinket?

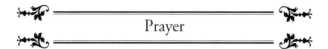

Prayer

Lord, allow me to become the woman You created me to be. Help me discover the tools needed to build my house and remove the ones I've used to tear it down. I bind lack and chaos in my house and I loose Your peace and prosperity. Teach me how to be a good steward over what You've given to me. In the name of Jesus, I pray. Amen.

Woe to him who builds his house by unrighteousness-
Jeremiah 22:13

Don't Be a Beautiful Sepulcher

Woe unto you, scribes, Pharisees and hypocrites! You are like white washed tombs, which indeed appear beautiful outward, but are within full of dead men's bones, and all uncleanness. Matthew 23:27

A sepulcher is a tomb, grave or burial place for the dead. At first glance, a sepulcher may leave you awestruck because of its beautiful artwork and statues - but in reality, everything inside it is fruitless - incapable of producing anything. When I heard the Lord say "beautiful sepulcher," in my spirit I knew exactly what He was telling me. I have allowed so many dead things to compile and take up space in my life until the anointing to speak life went ignored. I walked around being able to usher others into a place of peace, yet I was stuck tending to death inside me.

How many times do we walk around eloquently put together, dressed from head to toe, but inside of us are old dead hurts? We get all dolled up to walk around carrying decomposing, rotten pain. We begin to exercise, change our lifestyles and vow to not overeat, but the bones of bitterness reside in our members.

It is easy for us to recognize the turmoil that goes on in others, but we ignore the painstaking urges to confront our own demons. You have got to know that you are not fooling God by lifting your hands up every Sunday, crying at the altar for bible study or when you feed the homeless for the holidays! God knows our hearts. He knows what we need to hold on to and what we need to let go of. Remember, all good and perfect things come from Him, so the things you need to proceed are in Him.

I do not have a 12 step program for this, but I do know the first step is admitting that there's a struggle churning within to release the ghosts of your past. We can't deny or ignore the bad experiences that happened, nor can we overlook the fact that they caused us to set up negative emotions. The Word of God tells us to confess our faults, one to another and pray for one another, that we may be healed. The prayers of a righteous person is powerful and effective (James 5:16). It is acceptable to share with someone who genuinely wants to see you set free! God may use your current relationships to bless you and get you to truly understand who He is.

Sometimes we do everything humanly possible to be set free, but spiritually we must unlock the tomb. The beauty that is seen outwardly is to be a reflection of the life of Christ, not the deeds of the dead. Death has a stench that is recognized no matter how much fragrance you use. The most expensive oils and perfumes cannot mask the scent of low self-esteem and low self-worth. It does not neutralize the aroma of evil and it certainly cannot cover pain. I charge you today to start the path of healing by confessing, praying and receiving forgiveness for self and others.

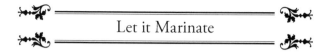

Let it Marinate

Should we place our dreams, goals and desires in the bowers of the tomb or do we recognize that we must speak life to dormant things and bury that which is dead? Therefore if any man be in Christ, he is a new creature: old things have passed away; behold all things are become new (II Corinthians 5:19-21).

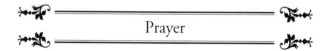

Prayer

Lord, I give You every unproductive thing in my life that You may revive it or remove it. If there is any dead thing that is weighing me down, I believe that You will take it away by faith. In the name of Jesus, I pray. Amen.

Therefore, if anyone cleanses himself from what is dishonorable, he will be a vessel for honorable use, set apart as holy, useful to the Master of the house, ready for every good work.
II Timothy 2:21

Put Things in Order

But seek first the kingdom of God and His righteousness, and all these things will be added to you. Matthew 6:33

We have so many things that demand our time. Some things are immediate, others are not as urgent, but they are important. Trying to put things in perspective can be challenging. Most youth have to decide what school they will attend, what trends are popular and how they will spend their weekend. Young adults have to decide what will be their career choice, where they will reside and whether or not they are satisfied with their choices. Parents have to shuffle work, extracurricular activities, the kids, the spouse or significant other and the house. Notice not one of those scenarios included "God time." We usually place Him last on the list when He should be first. Allow me to share the four F's that fuel our lives.

Family

Children look to their parents for their basic survival needs. We see no error in how our parents rear us and become more reliant on them as we grow older. If we have never built our own relationship with God as adults, we will continue to rely on our parent's prayers or faith to help us through. We call them for help or to make us feel better and when we can't reach them, we get upset.

Friends

Much like family, we develop trust and a bond with our friends. We tell them secrets and go years confiding in them and entrusting them with our possessions and personal space. When things go bad, we expect them to stick around. Again, we put our trust in a fallible person instead of the infinite power of God.

Finances

It is true; money answers all things, but it is also true that the love of money is the root to evil. The rat race to success will get us dizzy. In order to maintain, we must have realistic goals and allow our finances to match our current lifestyle. The moment we place one over the other, we create an imbalance that results in us always compensating to create a balance. Our money should never be our motivation. It should never make us lose sight of resources or replace our God.

Foolishness

This categorizes every "extra" thing that we get involved in. Foolishness consists of the things we can live without such as entertainment, sports, hobbies, social outings or shopping for things we really don't need. Whether it is recreational or therapeutic, it can become too consuming and wreak havoc on your spiritual growth. Sometimes we feel we must incorporate "down time" because the other three F's have taken up too much time.

Let it Marinate

Ponder on these things and remember - let nothing separate you from the love of God. We should always start any endeavor with the Lord, but when the demands of life get so urgent, we respond naturally to a present request. With God, these things are like puzzle pieces intricately put in place to create a whole, harmonious image. Let God help you to put things in order and when things get off track He can redirect you with His Word.

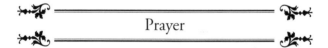

Prayer

Lord, quiet my mind and help me focus on You. Create an opportunity for me to evaluate my priorities and put things in order. My relationship with You and my family are very important to me, but I want to make sure that I am doing all I can to receive the best out of each. Teach me to be anxious for nothing, how to pray and how to put You first. In the name of Jesus, I pray. Amen.

Whoever pursues righteousness and kindness
will find life, righteousness, and honor.
Proverbs 21:2

Make a To Do List

The heart of man plans his way, but the Lord establishes his steps. Proverbs 16:9

In the course of the day our "to do" list is seldom completed no matter how much time and preparation we have made. Our grocery list is long, but we sometimes forget the bread. Our laundry list is tedious, but we forget the baskets or soccer uniform. No matter how many times we clean up, our chance to get that other closet in order is a faint memory.

Let us look at the "to do" list for our growth. Some people incorporate a bucket list or a wish list, but there are some things we need to do right now. Take a moment and think on your priorities from least to greatest. I have always heard two sayings that lets me know that we must put a lot of thought into what we do: (1) If you get the head right, the body must follow and (2) What is in the head flows to the body.

What we think about has a great deal to do with what we believe. In order to do anything, we must first believe that we can do something. Are you where you believe you should be financially? If not, why? If so, what's next? Are your children being reared the way you deem acceptable? If not, why? If so, how can you continue?

Two of the things that are always on my heart are my children and whether I am financially stable enough to make their lives better. Keep in mind that your "to do" list is subjective to your lifestyle and not that of another. Make sure that your list incorporates those things that are currently or presently active or helpful in your life now. Whatever you need to do, make sure you have counted up the costs and sacrifices in order to move forward.

Let it Marinate

We don't drift in good directions. We discipline and prioritize ourselves there. In order to realistically execute your "to do" list, you have to make shorter, attainable goals and not focus on what you do not have or lack. You must stop guilt in its tracks and never compare yourself to others.

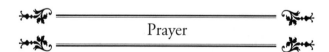

Prayer

Lord, help me to prioritize and declutter my life so that I may see and hear You clearly. If I'm wasting time on things and others, show me. I want my life to be full of purpose and please You. To whom much is given, much is required. In the name of Jesus, I pray. Amen.

> *The thoughts of the righteous are just;*
> *the counsels of the wicked are deceitful.*
> *Proverbs 12:5*

Wait on God

Wait for the Lord: be strong, and let your heart take courage; wait for the Lord! Psalm 27:14

For many years of my life, I have thought if I do this or that - things will get better. I came to the realization that my way is not always best. Most of my disappointments, bad judgments and wrong actions came from me not waiting on God. It sounds easier than it is, but it always begins with a thought - I can either wait or take matters in my own hand; or God won't move unless I do something. When I meditated on the Word, the instructions brought clarity. Psalm 40:1 reminds me that He heard my cry - now all I have to do is wait on Him!

I examine my life and say "nobody but God." He put me in the position where I knew that it was only Him who bought me through it. The times when the bills were due and the funds were low, He made a way. When the kids were sick or in trouble and I had to make a decision to work or tend to them, God provided and we never went without.

Waiting is an action - to be still until a specific time. It means being ready, yet it means to postpone. We must learn that waiting is temporal until our expectation is met. God wants us to be patient and expecting. We have to anticipate the wait in order to allow Him to have His way. When we react without waiting, we invent ideas or ways to fix issues. We will pray about the problem and still come up with our own resolution when we don't understand what God is doing.

Now I don't mind waiting - because when I wait, I know it is the will of God in the matter. I am passed the point of figuring stuff out while God is working. Waiting proceeds trusting and this in turn builds our faith. Waiting keeps us from repeating mistakes and premature conclusions. I wish I had learned this early on, but I am sure I would not be where I am now. My faith, income and relationships developed by waiting - but most importantly, I learned more about and from God by waiting.

Let it Marinate

My children come to me for just about every need that they have; field trips, extracurricular things, take me here, buy me that - and most times I tell them that they have to wait. While they are waiting, I'm making sure the funds are there, checking my schedule to see if I am off or who can I get to be proxy when I can't make it. This is the same thing that God is doing before He gives you the green light. He is configuring the process and as you continually ask, He is teaching you how to wait. My children trust that I'm going to come through. and they know that whatever they ask I am going to come through. God's children should be the same way.

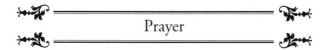

Prayer

Lord, I'm coming to You like a child knowing that You have my best interest in the palm of Your hands. Your Word says that You give Your best gifts to Your children. Teach me patience that I may not get weary while waiting and I will accept what You allow. In the name of Jesus, I pray. Amen.

The Lord is good to those who wait for Him,
to the soul who seeks Him.
Lamentations 3:25

Seasoning

/ see-zuh-ning /

The process of adding salt,
herbs, vegetables or spices
to enhance the flavor of the gumbo.

Examine Yourself

Search me, O God, and know my heart. Try me and know my thoughts; and see if there be any grievous way in me, and lead me in the way everlasting. Psalm 139:23-24

Mirrors are everywhere. We can look at ourselves in the mirror at the house, in the car or in any bathroom in the world. We stay there until the makeup is perfect, the hair is neatly coiffed and the outfit is fully set. We can clearly see our reflection on the outside, but we cannot see our reflection on the inside. What if we had a spiritual mirror that showed us what we looked like on the inside? Imagine having a spiritual MRI. It scans you anatomically, carefully searching for something foreign that could potentially do much damage. It searches out the real view of you. What would the MRI of your soul reveal - hidden secrets, regrets, poor choices, abuse, a foul and negative tongue, unhappiness, failure, success, depression, an impure heart, an unsound mind, fear, jealousy, envy, strife, lust or an unkempt temple?

When you look in the mirror, the outer appearance tells our past. The aging face, weight gain and scars are all results of where we've been. Just like the natural body deteriorates when it is not properly nourished or cared for, so does the spirit man. The image in the mirror reveals the things we can cover up or downplay, but the spiritual mirror searches the depths of our soul. What we see in it causes us to deal with things we choose to hide. The good thing about this mirror is that nobody sees this image but you and God. He created you, so He will allow you to see your strengths and weaknesses and give you the tools to transform. When it is complete, the inward transformation will produce an outward manifestation. Our spirit man will transform when we continually keep watch over it, purging familiarity and emotions that support fleshly desires and bad repetitive behaviors.

There is a desire in every believer to be more like Christ, but the clutter that we refuse to let go keeps us from it. We must always take inventory of our lives. We must accept the trials we go through. They bring joy and pain, but will help us to relinquish self and let God do the molding of our heart, mind, body or soul.

Let it Marinate

Examine yourselves, to see whether you are in the faith. Test yourselves. Or do you not realize this about yourselves, that Jesus Christ is in you?—unless indeed you fail to meet the test! I hope you will find out that we have not failed the test. (II Corinthians 13: 5-6)

Prayer

Lord, help me to examine my life. I want to love the image I see in the natural and the spirit. I want to accept what I can't change and reject what's untrue. Even though I've had a few bad experiences, I am perfect in Your sight. There are things that I've purposely overlooked, forgotten or chosen not to deal with. Today, I want to move forward. In the name of Jesus, I pray. Amen.

The Lord judges the peoples; judge me,
O Lord, according to my righteousness
and according to the integrity that is in me.
Psalm 7:8

Watch Your Mouth

For every kind of beast and bird, of reptile and sea creature, can be tamed and has been tamed by mankind, but no human being can tame the tongue. It is a restless evil, full of deadly poison. With it we bless our Lord and Father, and with it we curse people who are made in the likeness of God. From the same mouth come blessing and cursing. My brothers, these things ought not to be so. James 3: 7-10

Whoever created the misconception that words don't hurt has never met a child who has been bullied, a woman who has been emotionally or verbally abused by her parents when she was a child or a victim of domestic violence.

Words hurt, especially when they come from people we know, love and cherish. The bible says the tongue is a small part of the body but has a large impact (James 3:5). Think of the negative statements a parent, sibling, friend, family member, spouse or boss might have said to you -You're ugly. You're stupid. You are fat. You are an awful mother. I wish you were never born. You will never be good for nothing. You will never amount to anything. These words resonate in your mind years after they have been spoken and you can't seem to shut them out. Sometimes the words are spoken so frequently that you begin to think you're ugly, stupid and fat. You start to feel like you aren't a good mother, you don't have a purpose or you never will accomplish anything. Constantly being criticized and told you aren't good enough causes you to lose confidence and it lowers your self-esteem. As a result, you may start to blame yourself for the other person's abusive behavior.

Never underestimate the power of words. Proverbs 18:21 says that the tongue has the power of life and death. Verbal assaults may not cause physical damage, but they do cause emotional pain and scarring. Yelling is intimidating. Blaming exonerates and places blame on the innocent. Sarcasm sabotages conversations. Name calling belittles and devalues. Fault finding is negative criticism. Guilt trips are controlling and insults are used to overpower and lower self-esteem. The victim of abuse will constantly question what they did and who they are. Not only do they doubt the reason for their existence, but they begin to forget who God created them to be.

People who use their words to hurt, control, manipulate or intimidate are abusive. They are typically masking issues of inadequacy, jealousy, envy and insecurity. Abusers learn to abuse because they have been abused themselves or they have watched someone else get abused. Verbal assaults don't happen overnight. You go from being bae to bitch, honey to whore and sweetheart to stupid. They go from praising you to slandering you. It is not God's best for us to allow people to berate us and trample on our spirits. We can't continue to take the insults with a smile. After a while, we will get worn down and accept the lies of the enemy.

The key to conquer verbal assault is to replace it with God's truth. Speak the Word of God over your life. You are fearfully and wonderfully made. You are a child of God. No weapon formed against you shall prosper. You are the righteousness of God. You have a purpose. God has a good plan for your life!

Once you replace the lies with the truth, you must forgive the abuser. If you want to oppress the oppressor, forgive them and remove their power. Learning to forgive doesn't require you to forget or ignore the wrong, but it teaches you to love others with the love of Christ in spite of the harm they caused you. Be willing to forgive those who have sincerely repented and those who are not apologetic at all. God forgives you when you do wrong, but He doesn't remove the consequences. The same is true for the abuser; they will be forgiven, but they must deal with the consequences and repercussions of their words and actions. There is a great reward in forgiveness. It relinquishes us from vengeance and places our focus on what God has for us. The disparagement was sent to tear you down, but God came that you might have life in abundance.

Let it Marinate

Remember how you felt when someone spoke damaging words to you? It hurt. Don't become the person that hurts others with words. Govern your tongue to speak uplifting, encouragement to others. Lives and careers have been shaped by what comes out of the mouth. We all know what Dr. Martin Luther King's "I Have a Dream" speech did for mankind and the civil rights movement - on the other hand, let's not forget about the Paula Deen situation! Watch your mouth!

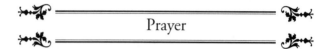

Prayer

Lord, teach me how to forgive those who have hurt me. Uproot the negative that has been planted in my mind and spirit and show me who I am in You. Father, I release those who have caused me pain and ask that You heal me from the inside out. In the name of Jesus, I pray. Amen.

With his mouth the godless man
would destroy his neighbor,
but by knowledge the righteous are delivered.
Proverbs 11:19

Check Your Motives

But if you have bitter jealousy and selfish ambition in your hearts, do not boast and be false to the truth. For where jealousy and selfish ambition exist, there will be disorder and every vile practice. James 3:14, 16

Check the motives of what you say. Most of the time when a person says they do not want to be mean or come across a certain way, it is usually followed by critique. There is absolutely nothing wrong with constructive criticism, but sometimes it may be destructive. Even if you were speaking the truth, it may hurt. Many relationships are severed by what someone said or how it was said. Think about a time when someone took what you said the "wrong way." What did you really mean? Were you tearing down or building up? Were you encouraging or discouraging? Were you helping or hurting? Whatever you said, God knows your heart; but remember that words have a tendency to create life or death. We should always be honest, but we should speak the truth in love. Sometimes our motives are misunderstood and the recipient takes offense to what was said. If our motives are pure, they will eventually get the revelation and accept that you meant well.

If the motivations behind your words are not pure, your true intentions will eventually be revealed. The bitterness, envy and selfish ambition in your heart will have long term effects on others, but you may not realize how it affects you. We are held responsible for every word we speak. If you sow negativity, you will reap negativity. You may not even realize the magnitude of animosity you have for a person until you open your mouth.

Check the motives of what you do. When we do things for people with a pure heart, we should always have the intention to give, not to receive. If you think about what you will get out of it first, you are doing it with impure intent and God is not pleased. Matthew 6:1 says that you should beware of practicing your righteousness before other people in order to be seen by them; for then you will have no reward from your Father who is in heaven. Bottom line: our purpose is to please God, not people.

We may be able to hide our true motives from other people, but we will never be able to hide them from God. He is the one who examines our hearts. Even if we spend our entire lives doing good deeds, we will reap a bitter harvest if we do or say things with an unclean heart. On the other hand, if our purpose is to please God, we will. Check your motives.

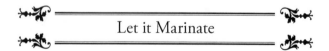

Let it Marinate

Words cut like a knife that passes through skin and bone and go straight to the heart. A skillful surgeon can work a knife to do good, but if you put that same knife in the hands of the wicked, it instantly becomes a weapon to do great harm. The same is true for words. What we say has the power to break someone's heart or put it back together.

Love cuts, then cleanses and covers a wound that God heals in time. Hate cuts, then infects and exposes the wound, causing it to heal improperly and disfigure. If we regularly examine the motives behind the things we anticipate saying or doing, we will avoid displeasing God and suffering the consequences that impure motives bring.

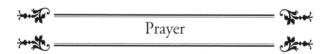

Prayer

Lord, if You find anything in my heart, mind or spirit that is not right, I ask that You remove it. Allow the fruits of Your Spirit to reside in mind, heart, body and soul. Show me how to see the good in others and encourage them to see what You see. If I have said or done anything to cause another to stumble, I repent. Build me up where I am torn down that I may bless others. In the name of Jesus, I pray. Amen.

The righteousness of the blameless
keeps his way straight,
but the wicked falls by his own wickedness.
Proverbs 11:5

Assess Your Friends

A man of many companions may come to ruin, but there is a friend who sticks closer than a brother. Proverbs 18:24

Friends – how many of us have them? The meaning of friendship has been watered down in its definition with each generation. The term "friend" is used so casually, I am inclined to believe that some people do not really know what a real friend is. What type of friends do you have? What type of friend are you?

True friendships have no gender, ethnicity or socioeconomic status and start with a common denominator. Friends often share likes, dislikes, interests, pursuits and passions, but friends can come from different backgrounds and have different views on life. Friends don't value one friend over the other, nor do they belittle or humiliate. A friend's love is there in spite of distance. When you cry, they cry and their pain is your pain. True friends take risks, overlooks faults and love unconditionally. Friends share thoughts and feelings without fear of judgment or negative criticism. They encourage one another and forgive when there has been an offense. They call out ungodly behaviors in others in love.

A real friend will not sit around and watch the other live destructively without showing concern. Even though they may be polar opposites, they do not want to see the other hurt. They share a sense of care and concern, a desire to see one another grow and develop, and a hope for each other to succeed in all aspects of life.

Friendships are complex because change is evitable. A friend who has a lot on their plate may not be able to be there for you physically, but they are prayerful and concerned about you. Sometimes we say "this is my friend until the end," but the end may not be the one you think it is. A friendship may end due to a relationship, career or spiritual choice. One friend may mature faster or the other is just simply ready for something new. God sometimes severs friendships that we may grow in Him.

There are some friends who are "friends with benefits". People often misconstrue this phrase to refer to people that are sexually or intimately involved, but the friends I am talking about are the ones who are a benefit to you and you are a benefit to them. They are the friends who have the right connections. They will get you off the hook when trouble comes or get you into any business network or social circle that you desire. You do not talk to these friends until you need them and it's ok because they know you will reciprocate the benefits in return! Friends with benefits do not mind chauffeuring you around, picking your kids up from school, running your errands or loaning you money. Again, this type of friendship is always mutually beneficial.

There are friends who are "prayer warriors". These are the people you call when all hell breaks loose or when you are going through a crisis. You call the prayer warrior when your back is up against the wall or a relationship has ended. You know they will always listen to you, pray for you and cry with you, even if you never return the favor.

God's Word tells us that a friend sticks closer than a brother and in order to be a friend, we must show ourselves friendly. True friendship exemplifies agape love. This love mirrors the love that comes from God. Jesus calls us His friends and He laid down His life for us. God wants us to have friends here on earth, but He also wants us to be friends with Him! Are you a friend of God?

Let it Marinate

Two are better than one; because they have a good reward for their labour. For if they fall, the one will lift up his fellow: but woe to him that is alone when he falleth; for he hath not another to help him up. Again, if two lie together, then they have heat: but how can one be warm alone And if one prevail against him, two shall withstand him; and a threefold cord is not quickly broken. Ecclesiastes 4: 9-12

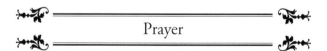

Prayer

Help me to be a genuine friend and show me the people that are not genuine. Teach me how to love others, even if I have to love them from a distance. I pray that all my relationships edify and strengthen me, but most importantly that they glorify You. In the name of Jesus, I pray. Amen.

> *One who is righteous is a guide to his neighbor,*
> *but the way of the wicked leads them astray.*
> Proverbs 12:26

Don't Fan the Flame

Besides that, they learn to be idlers, going about from house to house, and not only idlers, but also gossips and busybodies, saying what they should not. I Timothy 5:13

When tension gets thick or chaos fills the air, the first thought that comes to mind is "it's getting hot in here," especially when tempers begin to flare and both parties have a heated exchange with no resolve. In most cases, there is an instigator or "fire starter". They are the type of people who enjoy striking matches and watching things burn to the ground. In other words, fire starters get high or find pleasure in starting fires.

Just as this definition defines the literal fire starter, the same applies to the proverbial one. They will sow seeds of discord in marriages, relationships and friendships. Fire starters cannot resist the opportunity to tear someone down with their words or actions. They do this in an attempt to feel better about themselves and to see people at odds. The fire starter's main objective is to bring pleasure to their aching soul by watching your stuff go up in flames!

Your homework is to seek out the fire starters in your life and remove their tools. You can remove their power to ignite or incite a fire just by turning a deaf ear to the foolery or simply bringing light to their tactics. You also have the power to extinguish fires by not giving life to things they conjure up. Fire starters are rendered helpless when they have no wind to fan the flames of their destructive fires.

Let it Marinate

You have the peace of God when you remove vicious people from your life. This is a peace that surpasses all understanding. When you receive it, you will do everything in your power to protect it. This peace helps you to make clear decisions, seek wise counsel and establish healthy relationships. If you have digested this information and can't think of the fire starter in your life, it might just be you.

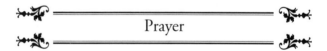

Prayer

Father, remove those that seek to destroy my relationships through manipulation and chaos. I pray for discernment to weed out the fire starters in my life. They might form a weapon, but thank God, it will not prosper. In the name of Jesus, I pray. Amen.

> *The righteous is delivered from trouble*
> *and the wicked walks into it instead.*
> Proverbs 11:8

Depart or Leave

And if the house is worthy, let your peace come upon it, but if it is not worthy, let your peace return to you. And if anyone will not receive you or listen to your words, shake off the dust from your feet when you leave that house or town. Matthew 10:14-15

Departure means the action of leaving, typically to start a journey. When you have made peace about a situation, job or a relationship, you have the ability to depart and walk away in confidence. You alert the source in a reasonable manner that you're headed in another direction. You learn from the situation and experience growth through the positive and negative interactions. You have peace about the situation because you did everything within your power to add value. You don't go around telling others that you are disgruntled, or do you pollute the minds of others as you depart. Those who are ready for a departure know that that their time has expired and it's time to move on.

When you leave, you do just that – leave. You don't have peace about leaving. You don't plan, pray or prepare. You give no warning and show no concern for the one you left behind. You walk away because you are fed up or upset, but when you calm down, it is a possibility that you may return to the place, person or situation you just left.

I watched a segment of a reality show where a wife left her husband and sons to go to another state with her boyfriend. The family heard from her periodically, but never received a true explanation on why she left. Of course, they knew she had a boyfriend, but they wondered if they had been 'that bad' of a family for her to abruptly flee. As the show progresses, I learned that her actions were the result of being left by her parents as a child. She was never given an explanation for why her parents left, so she didn't feel like she owed her family one either.

I am sharing this story because there is a paradigm concerning leaving and departing. Leaving denotes abandonment, unfinished business and assumptions. Departure denotes preparation, consideration and closure. If you are not pleased with a current aspect of your life, take the necessary steps to fix it or depart. If you don't like your salary, go back to school or get another job. If you don't like the state of your marriage, go get counseling or get a divorce. If your church is not changing you, change churches. No need to scream or cause a scene. Just depart.

Let it Marinate

The Word states that if peace doesn't abide, shake the dust from your feet and keep moving. Will you depart or leave?

Prayer

Lord, teach me how to handle situations decently and in order. If I have sabotaged relationships, teach me how to ask for forgiveness. Help me to make better choices when I depart from things that don't suit me anymore. In the name of Jesus, I pray. Amen.

Righteousness will go before Him and make His footsteps a way.
Psalm 85:13

Get Ready – Get Set – Wait

And let steadfastness have its full effect, that you may be perfect and complete, lacking in nothing. James 1:4

God said it is not good for man to be alone. There is no place in the bible where the word "single" can be found; a person was called unmarried or widowed. God created man and woman in His image, blessed them and told them to be fruitful and multiply. The two became one flesh to enjoy life and procreate. If you desire to be married, there are instructions on what to do while you are single. Get ready, get set and wait.

Phase 1: Get Ready

If you are called to do something, you will be in preparation mode for a period of time. Get ready means you must be willing to prepare yourself. You have to be ready to date before you seriously consider dating. You must be in a state of contentment with what you have, who you are and where you are going. You are focused on the will of God and His plan for your life. Get ready means that you are not actively looking to date anyone. You are busy getting your life, home and finances in order. You are fully aware that you do not need a mate to complete you, but you want one who will compliment you.

Phase 2: Get Set

After you have gone through the phase of preparation, it is time to get set. Get set means that you are settled in being ready. Spiritually, being set is God's way of keeping the unmarried from falling into temptation. It means to be settled in the mindset of being whole. At this point, God has you set or fixed on His will. You devote more time to the things and people of God. You set realistic goals and relationship expectations. Getting set does not mean that you settle or compromise your standards. You acknowledge God and respect yourself and your body because you are aware that everyone you meet is not dating or marriage material. When you are set, you can date according to Godly standards, your lifestyle and your speed.

Phase 3: Wait

Wait means to stay in place until an expected event happens, until someone arrives or until it is your turn to do something. To wait is to be in a hidden or concealed position or in a state or attitude of watchfulness. Get busy waiting! That sounds like an oxymoron to some, because they think that waiting means to do nothing. The spiritual aspect of waiting coincides with its true definition- to stay in place until an event happens, someone arrives or it's your turn. While you are waiting, you are doing what God has entrusted you to do and you are putting the things you've learned into practice. You are not looking for someone who goes to church, but someone who is the church. You are not looking for someone to save you, because Jesus already did that! The race isn't given to the swift or the strong, but to the one who endures. Get Ready. Get Set. Wait.

Let it Marinate

Getting ready is the process of sifting through the things you need to get set. You know what you want, what you don't want and you're patiently waiting for the unknown. Even if you never get the mate, you're still waiting on God. Wait, I say, on the Lord!

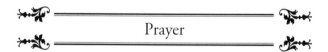

Prayer

The bible says that I should never be anxious for anything. I've found myself trying to force relationships and they have failed. Lord, show me how to wait. Bring women in my life to help bless my walk and show me why waiting is important. In the name of Jesus, I pray. Amen.

May integrity and uprightness preserve me,
for I wait for You.
Psalm 25:21

Meat

/ˈmēt /

The core of the gumbo;
A flavor enhancer to make
the gumbo hearty,
such as seafood, beef,
pork or chicken.

Get Over It

Jesus said to him, "Get up, take up your bed, and walk." And at once the man was healed, and he took up his bed and walked. John 5: 8-9

You may ask, "What if I never get over it?" Whatever "it" is certainly has a conclusion, but first you must find the cause of "it". Whether you choose to admit it or not, you are the sum of your choices. Where you are right now is because of the choices you have made. The career that you have is because of the education and/or training that you have received. The inmate is imprisoned because of a past offense.

Regardless if you have accepted God's gift of life or not, you still must face the consequences of the choices that you've made. Sickness will not be healed by singing in the church choir. The backlash of a dishonorable past is not erased by accepting Christ. Generational obscenities are not broken because you are called to ministry.

Is "it" hurt, sickness, rumors, shame, abuse or generational? It will paralyze us with fear, causing us to remain in situations that aren't benefiting us. It can be an addiction that we can't shake without counseling or confession. It can have us deluded into believing nobody else sees it and it doesn't affect anyone. It can be so bad or familiar that we just accept it as being a part of who we are.

The only way to survive "it" is to have faith in God. Scriptures throughout the bible speak of great defeats over sickness, war and sin by faith. Every person is given a measure of faith, and when faith is mixed with God's word, you will be made whole. Faith in God brings forgiveness, makes a sick body well and brings hope to those that are lost. Placing faith in people, circumstances or things will often disappoint you and give a false sense of defeat. But whatever "it" is needs addressing before "it" takes you out!

Let it Marinate

A man afflicted for 38 years was just laying there, possibly constricted. Because Jesus could tell he had been in that situation for a while, He asked the man the question of a lifetime. "Will you be made whole?" You would think a person unable to move for that long would say, "I can't. I've been this way too long!" But the man said if someone would put him in the water troubled by the Angel, that he would be made whole. God recognized his faith and told him to rise, pick up his bed and walk.

If you really want to get delivered from your current state of paralysis (spiritually, emotionally and mentally), you don't need to rely on the availability or willingness of another to do something for you. All you need to do is reach out to the only One who can do it! The legs that were once too weak, too incompetent and too frail are now strong enough to move you beyond the pain. Get over it - so you can get on with it!

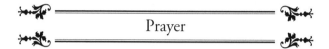

Prayer

Lord, I can't deny that the pain, hurt and shame of my situation is etched in my mind. The anger I have is too massive for me to explain, but today I'm coming to You like the man at the pool. I have no one to put me in and I feel powerless to do it myself. God, can You make me whole? Can You take this infirmity away that is eating away at my peace and joy? Can You strengthen me to walk without my issue? I'm ready to take up my bed and walk. I want to get over it. In the name of Jesus, I pray. Amen.

He restores my soul. He leads me in paths
of righteousness for His name's sake.
Psalm 23:3

Free Yourself

And you shall know the truth and the truth shall make you free. John 8:32

Harriet Tubman said "I freed a thousand slaves. I could have freed a thousand more if only they knew they were slaves." Oh my! How many times can we look over our lives and recognize when an open door was overlooked? We seem to have 20/20 vision in hindsight, but we are blindsided while we are in it. There are valid reasons why we stay bound. We stay bound in a marriage because of the kids or finances. We stay bound on the job because of location, salary and convenience. Whatever it is, there is an emotion attached that ties us there. Knowing you are bound is half the battle, but the key to break the chain is applying the knowledge. You have to know who you are, where you are going and what needs to happen to get there!

A person who has been abused can recognize an abuser. They have all of the information needed to assess the red signs of abuse, yet sometimes they enter into another relationship with an abuser.

A woman is kidnapped - her abductor tells her what to do and how to do it. He uses his power to demean, direct and disrespect her. She has accepted her situation and routinely adheres to the commands of her abductor. She is eventually freed, yet has a yearning to go back to what she had.

Different women, yet both are bound. Why? Because in their mind, they really don't know they are free. Some people spend their whole lives being a slave to others. These chains can only be broken through knowledge.

Let it Marinate

So a man thinketh, so is he. (Proverbs 23:7)

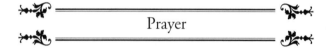

Prayer

Father God, I come to You believing that You will break every chain that is anchoring me to keep me from reaching my goals. I am free because Your Word says so. I am free because You paid the price for me. I am free because I believe it. In the name of Jesus, I pray. Amen.

Many are the afflictions of the righteous,
but the Lord delivers him out of them all.
Psalm 34:19

Keep Moving

I do not consider that I have made it my own. But one thing I do: forgetting what lies behind and straining forward to what lies ahead. Philippians 3:13

Everything is fast moving, but not always moving forward. When you drive a car, you occasionally have to look in the rearview mirror to see what is behind you. The rearview mirror can be a distraction if you use it to put on makeup or check your hair while you are driving. Those distractions can cause you to miss an exit, run a light or have an accident.

It is imperative that we understand the purpose of the rearview mirror in the journey of life. It helps us to see how far or close we are to a situation behind us. Sometimes, looking in the rearview mirror of life can cause fear, anxiety or depression - especially if you are focusing on old friendships, childhood issues, jobs or overlooked opportunities.

On the other hand, the rearview mirror can allow you to see how far God has brought you. He took some of us from darkness into the light. It shows us when we were sick, in need of healing and when we were perplexed, in need of deliverance. We cry tears of joy for our latter being greater. As we learn and get divine direction of purpose, we can proceed to our destination.

Press forward and keep moving ahead. Stop to refuel spiritually, mentally and emotionally. If you feel that you have lost your way, do not hesitate to ask God for directions. Once you reach your destination, you will see that all of the things in the rearview mirror facilitated in you getting where you are. The ride may have been rocky, but you made it!

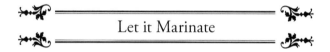

Let it Marinate

Remember Lot's wife? She escaped the destruction of the city, yet her heart and soul was in Sodom. Looking back caused her to lose her life. This is a clear example of your mind being in one place and body in another. She had no trust in what was ahead. She knew that the city would be burned, yet she longed to be in it. Her looking back spoke volumes, even to her husband. He was leading her to safety, but he witnessed her body object. The writer doesn't tell us why she looked back, but it does tell us that she turned into a pillar of salt when she did. Read Genesis 19:1-26

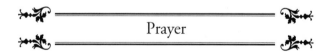

Prayer

Lord, I thank you that you allowed me to survive my past. I thank you for your protection even when I didn't know I needed it. Show me a more excellent way to distance myself from the things that have caused me harm. Change my desires and give me faith to trust in You and not look back. In the name of Jesus, I pray. Amen.

In the path of righteousness is life,
and in its pathway there is no death.
Proverbs 12:28

Get Well Soon

And behold, a woman who had suffered from a discharge of blood for twelve years came up behind him and touched the fringe of his garment, for she said to herself, "If I only touch his garment, I will be made well." Jesus turned, and seeing her he said, "Take heart, daughter; your faith has made you well." And instantly the woman was made well.
Matthew 9:20-22

We all know the story about the woman with the issue of blood. She used all of her resources, went to many doctors and never received a cure. Looking at it from another perspective, her issue of blood got her covered with The Blood! God healed her just by her faith. The ailment that bound her for 12 years made her an object of ridicule, shame and defeat. She was not allowed to touch or be touched. Our issues do the same. We cannot touch or be touched without affecting or being affected by those around us. Our family, friends, mates or coworkers become alienated because of the issue.

Despite what she knew, the woman was determined to be free of her infirmity. She set out on a quest that could have cost her her life. She spent all that she had, so she had nothing to lose. Her perplexing issue caused her to try one more time. She wanted to be washed in the blood, which was the same thing that caused her to have an "issue". She was determined to be made whole by any means necessary, so she pressed pass the crowd and received her healing. Whatever your issue is, you can be made whole and you can get well. The blood of Jesus never lost its power to cleanse, save, resurrect, or heal!

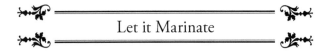

Let it Marinate

A bad marriage, horrible divorce, dysfunctional childhood, unspeakable pain or memories that haunt and taunt you cannot be given power. They have found a safe haven in your heart, mind and spirit. The aforementioned have arrested you for too long. It may not have been 12 years, but it has been long enough. A constant bleed depletes your energy, strength and ability to make sound judgment. Are you going to be like the crowd and just watch God do something for everyone else or will you push through and touch Him so that you can be whole? Do you want to be covered or bleed out? Choose wisely and get well soon.

Prayer

Father God, my issue has gone on too long and I am weak. I have spent much and done even more to try and rid myself of this infirmity. I don't want to cause anyone to become contaminated. I believe according to Your Word that I am healed. If I need professional help, Lord please send me to the right place and the right people. I will no longer walk around in agony, but I accept my healing this day. My faith is in You that I will never have to cower in shame, but will hold my head high in victory. In the name of Jesus, I pray. Amen.

For your name's sake, O LORD, preserve my life!
In your righteousness bring my soul out of trouble!
Psalm 143:11

Father Forgive Them

And Jesus said, "Father, forgive them, for they know not what they do." And they cast lots to divide his garments. Luke 23:34

Everyone has been hurt by the actions or words of another. Perhaps your parents criticized your parenting skills, your coworker ruined a project or your partner had an affair. These wounds can leave you with lingering feelings of anger, bitterness or even vengeance. If you don't practice forgiveness, you might be the one who pays most dearly. By embracing it, you can also embrace peace, hope, gratitude and joy that leads you down the path of physical, emotional and spiritual well-being. When you have been hurt by someone you love and trust, you might become angry, sad or confused. If you dwell on past hurts, grudges filled with resentment, vengeance and hostility can take root. If you allow negative feelings to crowd out positive feelings, you might find yourself swallowed up by your own need to be forgiven!

As children we heard about "sticks and stones may break my bones, but words will never hurt me." As adults we learned that it was the biggest rhyming fable ever told. Words hurt, actions hurt and we become bruised. How do you forgive them? You can forgive them very easily, especially when you know it's not about you, but about your mission. The ones closest to Jesus betrayed Him and denied they were tight with Him in fear of facing the same fate as Him. They didn't realize what they did to help Him fulfill His destiny from birth. From the moment Mary conceived Jesus, it was about forgiving people who were against Him from the start.

The Word says before you were a seed in your father's loins, He knew who you were! He knew the things that would scar you, scrape you and almost take you out. But He also knew that His plan was to prosper you, grow you and mature you to a person of faith that knows whatever happened was for your good. No longer can we walk around bleeding from old wounds. We can't let people see how we have allowed bad people and situations define who we are; or let everybody know just how angered we are by what someone did in our childhood, marriage or on the job. God's countenance should be upon you, He can't put something new in an old domain because contamination is eventual.

At the last moments of His life, Jesus said "Father, forgive them". He wasn't just talking about those who were persecuting Him. He was including the past, present and future! He went to the cross to forgive His enemies and your enemies that spoke evil against you and told lies that hurt you to the core. Your finances may never recover, your diagnosis may be permanent and you may NEVER get an apology from your adversaries, but it's your job to forgive them, because they do not know what they do.

Let it Marinate

If you never get an apology or redemption from those who hurt you will you always hold on to the hurt? Your pain is real, but your forgiveness will heal. Jesus taught us that their finite minds could not comprehend the magnitude of their actions. They helped fulfill the Promise on the Cross. Though they tried it, it worked out for your good. Forgive them

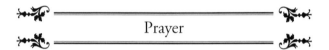

Prayer

Lord, I've held on to this for too long, for it has truly set up some emotions that are not good. My peace and joy have been held up because I can't allow myself to let go of the things that have caused me great pain. Teach me how to forgive like You, but most importantly teach me how to love like You. In the name of Jesus, I pray. Amen.

Vindicate me, O Lord, my God, according to your righteousness, and let them not rejoice over me!
Psalm 35:34

Still Here

And the princes, governors, and captains, and the king's counselors, being gathered together, saw these men, upon whose bodies the fire had no power, nor was an hair of their head singed, neither were their coats changed, nor the smell of fire had passed on them. Daniel 3:27 KJV

We've heard the story of the three Hebrew boys; how they wouldn't serve the king's god and were thrown in the fire. In astonishment, the crowd watched as the heat turned up and the men were unchanged! Shedrach, Meshach and Abed-Nego had no idea that on this day their faith would be tested, nor that their lives would be at stake- but yet they were certain of who their God was. The bible never speaks of their panic or wavering, but it does speak of their confidence in the Most High God. Had God come through for them before? Had they heard His voice or were they doing this to defy the order of the king? What on earth would make them have the assurance that their God would help them escape death? The truth is, they exercised their faith in a God they knew would never fail them or leave them. The story continues where the people witnessed the fourth man in the fire.

This is what I know about trials - you're either in one, going through one or just coming out of one. Your outcome determines how you fight and who you have fighting for you. As people look upon your situation, some hope you make it - while others are wish you wouldn't. As the heat gets hotter, you should remain calm - knowing that the fourth man is subject to show up at any time!

God will allow you to navigate alone for a while to see which route you will take. When He sees His child in trouble, He hurriedly executes His rescue plan. He allows you to take the excruciating pain of persecution, ridicule and feeling of abandonment. The smoke clouds your way but it never stops the fourth man from being visible to others. Your "going through" is not just about you, but those that are looking on. Even the naysayers have to agree that your God is mighty when they take note of your strength and ability to come out smelling like roses instead of smoke. The Word further tells us that the king not only charged the people to believe in their God, but He promoted them! Your circumstance will not only allow others to see God, but it will leave you better off. How many times have you been in a bind that only God could fix? How did those around you react and were blessed by the outcome? This passage is simple reminder that God is still here.

Let it Marinate

The bible said if you make your bed in hell He will be there also. That situation for those three boys was like hell! The heat was so hot that the two men that prepared them for the fire died from it. But God showed up! Nothing is too intense for Him to enter into your life. You can't do this alone. Let Him in.

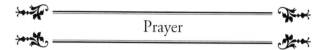

Prayer

Thank You for sharing my burden and lightening my load. You prepared a table in the presence of my enemies and I thank You for being with me while I go through and bringing me through in advance. I pray that others see You and are blessed by this. In the name of Jesus, I pray. Amen.

Behold, I long for your precepts;
in your righteousness give me life.
Psalm 119:40

Shine Your Light

Whatever you do, work heartily, as for the Lord and not for men. Colossians 3:23

Have you ever met a person that is a local icon, celebrity or activist? Someone who, where ever they go is recognized? They have a good rapport with their peers, they are revered by leaders and admonished by their elders! They are helpful in the schools, in the community and at church. They are a force to be reckoned with and a lover of all things harmonious. This "reluctant star" may be your friend, mother, sister or family member or maybe it is you! Whomever it is, their shoes are tough to walk in, their plate is always full and they are normally being emptied out with no replenishment in sight.

The blessing and the curse of being a reluctant star comes full circle. The blessing comes in the form of seeing others in a good place, resolving conflicts or just being there for someone in need. It is a blessing to be looked upon as a trailblazer or even a revolutionist and at the end of the day you go to bed with a sense of peace. The curse is that the weight becomes overwhelming at times. Although the reluctant star is able to advise others on love and life, she may go home alone. They are helping others to unearth painful secrets, yet they are keeping secrets. They are helping others mend relationships and theirs are in ruins.

The reluctant star is sometimes an insecure, shattered shell existing solely on the need to be needed. Her life has always been to please and ease the lives of others, often never thinking of what makes her happy, what makes her tick or what gives her peace. Whether she likes it or not, her actions are judged or watched by an audience of known and unknown critics. No matter what has transpired, she manages to keep a reassuring smile, even when she is clueless to what is next. The reluctant star is the chosen. God saw fit to distribute the weight on her broad shoulders, strengthened her muscles for the journey and equipped her with the tools needed for the task!

Let it Marinate

To whom much is given, much is required and the one who houses much wisdom is plagued with much sorrow. The joy of the Lord is her strength and without Him, she shall never know true peace, genuine love and extreme contentment! This should help you understand her. Shine bright, the spotlight is on you. It's show time all the time.

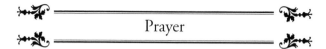

Prayer

God, I thank you for entrusting me with much. I believe that as I take care of Your people, You will take care of my affairs. I trust that Your favor is upon me to carry out the work. I accept it humbly with Your help that You will lead me into purpose. In the name of Jesus, I pray. Amen.

Then my tongue shall tell of your righteousness
and of your praise all the day long.
Psalm 35:28

Conclusion

And the Spirit and the bride say, Come. And let him that hears say, Come. And let him that is thirsty come. And whoever will… Revelation 22:17

"And whoever will" specifies that ANYONE who recognizes the need to "come" should come. This invitation to Christ isn't ceremonial, religious or a ritual. This invitation is a revelation-understanding that "whoever" needs to have a relationship with God can have it. Your sins or transgressions don't matter, your failures and disappointments are null and what you did prior to reading this book doesn't matter!

The only thing that matters is that you surrender your will to Him and believe the events that led up to the cross, the burial and the resurrection that revealed the risen Savior having all power. The plan of salvation is simply the acceptance of knowing that Jesus was born to die that you may live; that Jesus took away your sins that you can be free of them; that Jesus can do for you what you could never do for yourself.

You may have followed Jesus Christ before, "done everything right," yet things still didn't turn out how you thought they should- so you abandoned your faith and your relationship with Him. His word says that He would never abandon you even if you left Him. He would always be in the same place waiting to accept you.

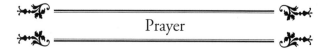

Prayer

Lord, I acknowledge that I'm a sinner and I confess that you are the Savior. I believe that You knew me before I was formed in the womb. I believe that You were conceived by the Holy Spirit, born of a virgin, died in the flesh and rose as the Christ. Come into my heart and remove the stones. Forgive me of all unrighteousness for Your name's sake. I desire to be reconciled to You as my Lord and my Savior and I vow to acknowledge you in all that I do. Amen

About the Author

Naisha Cooper is an ordained minister, entrepreneur and author. For over a decade, Naisha has been on a mission to reach the lost and reaffirm the called. She has ministered to the hearts and souls of others and shares an incredible testimony of perseverance in the midst of adversity. By the grace of God, Naisha has emerged with joy, strength and victory to effectively reach the masses with a message of hope in Jesus Christ through social media, books and community outreach. Naisha is a mother of three children - D'Henrei, Dacien and A'naisha.

To contact Naisha Cooper, please visit her website
www.NaishaCooper.com

Social Media
www.facebook.com/IamNaishaCooper
www.instagram.com/IamNaishaCooper
www.twitter.com/IamNaishaCooper

Printed in the United States
By Bookmasters